IN HER OWN TIME

ODETTE CHURCHILL

Catharine Sanders

Hamish Hamilton
London

Extract from Third Supplement to
THE LONDON GAZETTE
of Friday, the 16th of August 1946
CENTRAL CHANCERY OF THE ORDERS OF KNIGHTHOOD,

St. James's Palace, S.W.1.

20th August, 1946.

The KING has been graciously pleased to award the GEORGE CROSS to:
Odette Marie Céline, Mrs. SANSOM, M.B.E.,
Women's Transport Service (First Aid Nursing Yeomanry.)

Mrs. Sansom was infiltrated into enemy-occupied France and worked with great courage and distinction until April, 1943, when she was arrested with her Commanding Officer. Between Marseilles and Paris on the way to the prison at Fresnes, she succeeded in speaking to her Commanding Officer and for mutual protection they agreed to maintain that they were married. She adhered to this story and even succeeded in convincing her captors in spite of considerable contrary evidence and through at least fourteen interrogations. She also drew Gestapo attention from her Commanding Officer on to herself saying that he had only come to France on her insistence. She took full responsibility and agreed that it should be herself and not her Commanding Officer who should be shot. By this action she caused the Gestapo to cease paying attention to her Commanding Officer after only two interrogations. In addition the Gestapo were most determined to discover the whereabouts of a wireless operator and of another British officer whose lives were of the greatest value to the Resistance Organization. Mrs. Sansom was the only person who knew of their whereabouts. The Gestapo tortured her most brutally to try to make her give away this information. They seared her back, with a red hot iron and, when that failed, they pulled out all her toe-nails. Mrs. Sansom, however, continually refused to speak and by her bravery and determination, she not only saved the lives of the two officers but also enabled them to carry on their most valuable work.

During the period of over two years in which she was in enemy hands, she displayed courage, endurance and self-sacrifice of the highest possible order.

IN HER OWN TIME

This series focuses a spotlight on women whose lives and work have all too often been overlooked yet who have made significant contributions to society in many different areas: from politics and painting to science and social reform.

Women's voices have in the past been the silent ones of history. In Britain, for example, the restrictions of society, the time-consuming nature of domestic work, and the poor educational opportunities available to women until this century, have meant that not only did women rarely have the opportunity to explore their abilities beyond those which society expected of them, but also that their aspirations and achievements were often not recorded.

This series profiles a number of women who, through a combination of character and circumstance, were able to influence ideas and attitudes or contribute to the arts and sciences. None of them were alone in their ambitions. There must have been many other women whose experiences we know nothing of because they were not recorded. Many of the 'ordinary' women who have supported the so-called 'exceptional' women of history also displayed great courage, skill and determination. Political and social change in particular, has been accelerated by the pioneering work of individual women but rarely achieved without the collective efforts of masses of unknown women.

The work of many women in the series took them into the public eye: some were honoured and celebrated, more frequently they faced disapproval or lack of sympathy with their ideas. Many were ahead of their time and only later did their pioneering activities gain public respect. Others found their lives so deeply entangled with current events that their path was virtually chosen for them. A few were not closely involved with contemporary society but highly original characters who nevertheless influenced or informed others. By exploring the struggles, hopes, failures and achievements of these women, we can discover much about the society they lived in and how each made her personal contribution — in her own way, in her own time.

Olivia Bennett

The author and publishers would like to thank
Odette Hallowes
for telling us her story.

HAMISH HAMILTON CHILDREN'S BOOKS

Published by the Penguin Group
27 Wrights Lane, London W8 5TZ, England
Viking Penguin Inc., 40 West 23rd Street, New York, New York 10010, U.S.A.
Penguin Books Australia Ltd, Ringwood, Victoria, Australia
Penguin Books Canada Ltd, 2801 John Street, Markham, Ontario, Canada L3R 1B4
Penguin Books (N.Z.) Ltd, 182–190 Wairau Road, Auckland 10, New Zealand

Penguin Books Ltd, Registered Offices: Harmondsworth, Middlesex, England

First published in Great Britain 1989 by
Hamish Hamilton Children's Books
Copyright © 1989 by Catharine Sanders

Design by Sally Boothroyd
Cover design by Clare Truscott
Maps by Martin Ursell

British Library Cataloguing in Publication Data

CIP data for this book is available from the British Library

ISBN 0-241-12575-8

Typeset in Palatino by Butler & Tanner Ltd, Frome, Somerset
Printed in Great Britain by Butler & Tanner Ltd, Frome, Somerset

Contents

An Ordinary Woman

Real people are not heroes. Circumstances sometimes make heroes.

Phillipe Daudeny, introducing The Sorrow and the Pity, *a film about the occupation of France, made in 1969.*

In October 1942, a young Frenchwoman landed secretly on the coast of France, with a suitcase in her hand and a 'suicide' poison pill in her pocket. It was three years since the outbreak of the Second World War. Odette Sansom, French by birth but married to an Englishman, had come to fight the Nazis on French soil. From a quiet life as a wife and mother she had become a secret agent, her task to organise, train and arm French Resistance groups against the day when Allied armies would land once again in France.

She proved to be daring, ingenious and cool-headed. Betrayed after six months by a double agent, she was in German hands for two years and refused — even under torture — to give away information about other agents. She survived starvation, brutal interrogation and finally solitary confinement in the prison of the infamous Ravensbrück concentration camp.

Living under sentence of death, she drew from some inner source the strength to endure all these hardships without being either broken or embittered. Out of a number of female agents who survived the war, she became a celebrated heroine, yet she has never been willing to be thought unusual. Now in her late seventies, she says, 'I often think my story is impossible. I went to France an ordinary woman and I came back an ordinary woman — it was the events around me which were so extraordinary.' When Germany finally collapsed in 1945, and many prisoners were murdered, Odette escaped from Ravensbrück by what seemed like chance. She returned to England and her three children, and slipped back as quickly as she could into everyday family life.

In her two years in prison, Odette witnessed much evil and much good. During the long months of solitary confinement, she thought deeply about cruelty and suffering, and about human courage and endurance. Her story reveals a remarkable spirit, one which survived intact and never lost faith in humankind.

My comrades, who did far more and suffered far more profoundly, are not here to speak. Because of this I speak for them.

Odette

Chapter Two

Growing up in France

Odette Marie Céline was born on 28 April 1912. She was the eldest child of Gaston and Yvonne Brailly, a young couple living comfortably in Amiens, northern France. The plains of Picardy, where her childhood was spent, were to be one of the bloodiest battlefields of the First World War.

Odette was two when war with Germany broke out. Two years later, she and her younger brother Louis heard how their father, twice decorated for bravery, had been killed in action. Her mother was left to bring up two children on a small war pension, and they moved in with her parents-in-law. By 1918 the Germans had been defeated, but France was exhausted by the effort.

Odette's grandfather, a retired naval officer, took over the children's upbringing. He was a great believer in discipline and strength of character. Odette, who was terrified of the dark, was often made to go down the garden at night to fetch his spectacles. This was one of many tests designed to build up her courage.

An uneasy peace

Every Sunday, after church, her grandfather would take Odette and Louis to visit their father's grave. 'In twenty years,' he used to say, 'there will be another war. And you two will have to do your duty just as your father did.' His words made a deep impression on the children. He was not alone in his fears, for many other French people felt the same. The victorious general Marshal Foch warned, 'This is not a peace, it is a twenty-year armistice,' sensing that even though Germany was defeated, it could not be kept down for ever. Yet

One of the mass graveyards in France from the 1914–18 war, in which over seven million people lost their lives in battle and more than thirteen million were injured. This terrible legacy meant that Britain and France would go to any lengths to avoid another war.

much the victors did might have been designed to provoke the Germans into fighting again. In 1918, a British minister promised: 'We will squeeze Germany till the pips squeak,' and the harsh terms of the peace treaty contributed to the destruction of German industry and wild inflation which destroyed jobs and savings. This economic chaos encouraged millions of humiliated Germans, disillusioned with a weak government, to follow Adolf Hitler, the bitterest of them all. Already in 1919, ex-corporal Hitler was helping to build a National Socialist German Workers (Nazi) party, based on his fanatical conviction that Germany's defeat and economic distress were due to her betrayal by Jews and Communists.

Germany was also convinced it needed more 'lebensraum' (living space) to provide the vital raw

Ich bin Jude aber ich will mich nicht über die Nazis beschweren

▲ *The first decrees against Jews begun in 1928. Later they were banned from schools, universities and certain professions. Their synagogues were burnt, their shops vandalised and many people beaten up. This lawyer was forced to carry a placard saying, 'I am a Jew. But I will no longer complain about the Nazis.'*

◄ *Inflation in Germany rose so sharply after the First World War that at one time there were 43 million German marks to the pound. When the cash register in this Berlin grocery shop got too small, the owner had to use a tea chest to fit all the money in.*

materials for industry, which its competitors Britain and France could get from their many colonies. In the First World War Germany had been successfully blockaded and 'starved out'. To prevent this ever happening again, it was determined to expand its frontiers and increase its self-sufficiency in food and minerals.

Illness

While all this was going on in Europe, Odette was undergoing her own trials. Aged seven, she caught polio, for which there was no known treatment. She had to lie on her back, hardly moving, for nearly a year. Her grandfather did all he could to strengthen her spirit and sustain her optimism. 'I was very lucky,' she remembers, 'because he never let me feel sorry for myself. He taught me, even at that age, to accept what comes and make the best of it.'

11

Adolf Hitler was born in Austria in 1889 and volunteered to fight with the German army in 1914. By 1933 he was Chancellor of Germany.

Soon after her recovery from polio, Odette went blind. Her grandfather and the rest of her family filled her long, dark hours with stories, music and poetry, which Odette stored up in her mind. Specialists could neither explain nor cure her blindness and, in desperation, Yvonne took her to a herbalist. He made up an evil-smelling herbal mixture which eventually worked. This long illness had cut her off from school and friends, but Odette was not unhappy and remained especially close to her brother.

Marriage

The family moved to Boulogne in 1926, and there, when she was just seventeen, Odette met Roy Sansom. He was the young son of a British officer whom her grandmother had nursed during the war. They got engaged when she was eighteen, and Roy not much older, and married the following year. Odette, with her sheltered life and convent education, was really too young for marriage, as she soon discovered, but she was determined to do her best.

They stayed in France for two years and had a daughter, Françoise. Then Odette decided it would be better for Roy to return home, even though this meant leaving her family. They arrived in London in 1933. Odette knew no one and didn't speak a word of English, but eventually settled into the usual life of a full-time mother. Lili was born in 1934 and Marianne followed two years later.

The approach of war

The next few years were overshadowed by the Great Depression and the fear of imminent war with Germany. It had taken Hitler only twelve years to reach the centre of German politics. At first, Britain and France were too absorbed in their own economic troubles to pay close attention to events in Germany. But after becoming Chancellor in 1933, Hitler forced himself upon their notice. He embarked on a bitter persecution of the Jews and began, in defiance of the peace treaty, to re-build a powerful army, navy and air force and to annex neighbouring countries.

Odette watched anxiously as her grandfather's prophecy of another war seemed to be coming true. Hitler occupied the Rhineland, annexed Austria and threatened Czechoslovakia. The French and British, haunted by the millions of deaths in the last war, lacked the will to stop him. They refused to believe that anyone could want to repeat that destruction and failed to see that Hitler was intent on dominating Europe. These were the years of 'appeasement', when other countries repeatedly gave way to Hitler's pressure in the hope of satisfying him. It only encouraged him to make further demands.

The cartoonist David Low shows Hitler as a cross between Father Christmas and an evil giant from a fairy story. The children he is grabbing represent all the European countries he intends to dominate. The sack is labelled 'Germany above all others'.

13

EUROPE 1939

By September 1938, when he moved against Czechoslovakia, war seemed inevitable. In England air raid trenches were dug and gas masks issued for babies like Marianne. But at Munich, the British and French Prime Ministers forced the Czechs to surrender a large part of their country to Germany, rather than risk invasion and full-scale war. Hitler announced that he had no further territorial demands in Europe and Neville Chamberlain, the British Prime Minister, returned to England to cheering crowds who felt they had been reprieved from a death sentence. 'It is peace in our time,' he told them triumphantly. But the reprieve was short-lived. Six months later Hitler annexed the rest of Czechoslovakia. Britain and France responded at last, and guaranteed to defend Poland, clearly the next country threatened by Germany.

Chapter Three

War

We, the German Führer and Chancellor and the British Prime Minister ... regard the agreement signed last night and the Anglo-German Naval Agreement as symbolic of the desire of our two peoples never to go to war again.

From the document signed by Hitler and Chamberlain before war was declared

Preparations for war began in earnest. Odette, like the rest of the population, put up 'blackout' curtains, saw the sandbag defences piling up in the streets, and watched pregnant women, mothers and children leaving for the safety of the countryside. She decided to stay put. On 1 September 1939 news came that Hitler had

▶ *A soldier on leave says goodbye to his son. During the evacuation thousands of children were sent away from the cities to safer homes in the countryside. Some never saw their families again until the war ended.*

◀ *Neville Chamberlain on his return from Munich triumphantly holds up the 'No More War' document for the crowd to see Hitler's signature. Many believed, as he did, that war between the two countries had been averted.*

15

invaded Poland. After the months of tension, it was almost a relief to hear Chamberlain announce, two days later, that Britain and France were at war with Germany. Immediately the as yet unfamiliar air raid siren wailed its warning over London and silver barrage balloons rose into the sky.

The excitement did not last. It was a long, dark winter — a period known as the 'phoney war'. Many evacuees drifted back. Rationing began. Young men disappeared into the forces. Roy was called up. For those left at home like Odette, it was a dreary and frustrating time.

France falls

In April 1940, without warning, the Germans invaded neutral Denmark and Norway. In May, they stormed through Holland and Belgium, also neutral, heading for France. It was a totally unexpected attack — a Blitzkrieg or 'lightning war'. Holland fell in four days, Belgium in three weeks. German tanks and planes cut through the French armies, driving civilian refugees ahead of them. France was defeated in seven weeks. Odette wondered despairingly how the army of which her father had been so proud, could crumble so easily. Her mother and brother were caught up in the disaster as Boulogne, her home town, was captured.

After the British retreat from Dunkirk in May, France was forced to sign an armistice on 22 June. Feelings on both sides of the Channel ran high; the French felt Britain had abandoned them, the British felt France had lost the will to fight. Once, a London greengrocer, finding out that Odette was French, refused to serve her.

New jobs for women

The Battle of Britain then began, for the Germans knew they must first destroy Britain's RAF before risking an invasion. There was nothing phoney about the war now. Half the men between the ages

Paris in June 1940 was a city veiled in black. Thick clouds from burning petrol dumps masked the blinding summer sky. Houses disgorged their contents into all kinds of vehicles; furniture, possessions and people were hidden under pyramids of mattresses. Dogs were killed to save food. It was a case of every man for himself, with whatever he could salvage in all its sadness ...

... Old people piled into perambulators, were pushed along by weeping women, the children trailing after them, stupefied by the heat ... The ministries were moving, the tradesmen were shutting their shops. It was all over. There was already a sense of armistice about the abandonment of Paris. You hoped for an earthquake that you might escape the shame.

Marie Madeleine Fourcade, Noah's Ark

of twenty and twenty-five were in the forces. Women were volunteering too, for the Auxiliary Territorial Service (ATS), the Women's Royal Naval Service (the Wrens) and the Women's Auxiliary Air Force (WAAF). They released servicemen to fight and took on their skilled, heavy and dangerous jobs. Women controlled barrage balloons, worked on anti-aircraft gun sites, operated harbour boat services and drove heavy lorries and ambulances. Women pilots delivered aircraft from the factories to the squadrons.

The Second World War was a good time for women. I made a few bob. Men didn't like all these women working. On munitions the women would rush about getting extra money and it would be more than the husbands.

Lily Jane, What Did You Do in the War Mum?

Girls from the ATS in full battledress manning a range-finder at a gun emplacement. Women in the forces were allowed to do everything but press the trigger. Only Soviet women soldiers carried weapons to fight in the front line.

Looking back on it the Land Army work was hard, dangerous and dirty. But while the men were fighting we were doing what we could. Most of us felt like that. War work certainly made many women independent for the first time. Suddenly you could earn your own money and spend it how you wished. We had more freedom. We could go to the pictures by ourselves or go to dances.

Mrs Crane, What Did You Do in the War Mum?

As the call-up continued, women increasingly took on men's jobs in civil life, too. They took over responsible positions in local government, the Civil Service and 'essential' industries. They worked in munitions factories (and chalked rude messages to Hitler on the shells they produced). They trained as skilled mechanics, tool fitters and aircraft workers. They joined the land army and became farm labourers. They drove buses and became bank clerks. Many enjoyed the financial independence, companionship and new-found skills these jobs brought them. But the hours were long, and the work could be physically draining and monotonous. Many working women also faced the double burden of keeping families clothed and fed, at a time when everything was in short supply. However, despite the hardships or disadvantages, most women found war work gave them a taste of freedom and increased confidence.

Nothing that a woman can do, or can learn to do, should be allowed to absorb a man of military age.

Ernest Bevin, Minister of Labour, 1943

When the local milkman was called up, fifteen-year-old Rose Brown of Walworth took over his job. Many women who, on marriage, had been forced to leave jobs like teaching, nursing or in government service before the war, now found their skills in demand again.

A London bomb crater. One night 250 German bombers dropped nearly 400 tons of bombs within sixteen kilometres of Trafalgar Square.

Gray was [the colour of war] — all the fog-gray, sea-gray of rubble, of endless English days . . . gray in faces, especially of women . . . tired gray dirty arms, fatigue-gray. All other colour I remember is in contrast to this basic dim twilight gray of the war.

Mary Lee Settle, All the Brave Promises

The Blitz

By mid-August, Britain seemed to be winning the battle in the air. Unable to destroy the RAF, Hitler decided to bomb the population of London into submission. On 7 September, the Blitz began. By mid-November over 10,000 people had been killed. Every night exhausted Londoners tried to sleep in underground stations, as above them buildings collapsed and fires raged. By the end, one in six Londoners had lost their homes.

After a month of the Blitz, Odette removed her children to the safety of a small Somerset village. As a foreigner, she knew she might be unwelcome. It was lonely at first, but once the children went to the local school, the villagers befriended them. During that winter and the following spring,

JOAN BULL takes the BISCUIT!

and needs it too. Weston biscuits help her to carry on her countless jobs, whether in the Services or on the land, in factories, in hospitals, or keeping the home going.

They are concentrated energy-food, and the finest ingredients obtainable —wheat, sugar and fats—are used by Weston, the largest makers of biscuits in the Empire.

walking through the fields and woods and getting to know the people, Odette at last came to feel herself part of England, at home and secure. She had become very busy, nursing her mother-in-law, who died of cancer in the winter of 1941.

Behind enemy lines

Odette emerged from these private preoccupations to find that the war had changed. Britain was no longer struggling to prevent invasion by an unstoppable enemy. There was hope of victory. But to win the war, Britain had to get back into occupied Europe, to fight the Germans there and prepare the population to welcome and help the Allies when they invaded. French morale was recovering and resistance groups were beginning to fight back using guerilla tactics against the Nazis.

Early in 1940, the Special Operations Executive (SOE) was set up to recruit men and woman who could work behind enemy lines in Europe. They were to 'set Europe ablaze' by training and working with local units of resistance. They would sabotage factories, power stations and railways. Their activities would be a constant irritant to the Germans and a reminder of the British intention to liberate Europe from Nazi occupation.

The SOE urgently needed secret agents who spoke perfect French, knew the country and could pass unnoticed in occupied France. They found some of their agents by rather unorthodox methods. In the spring of 1942, Odette heard a radio broadcast in which the War Office requested photos and postcards showing the European coastline, in order to build up detailed knowledge. She sent off some family snapshots of her brother playing on the beach at Boulogne and thought no more of it. She didn't realise that the War Office had an ulterior motive — they were on the look-out for possible agents as well as pictures.

Chapter Four

A Change of Identity

To her surprise, Odette was invited to the War Office. It soon became clear that they were more interested in her than in her photographs. Would she be willing to do some war work, they wanted to know. 'Of course,' she responded, 'anything which doesn't take me away from my children.' At a second interview, Odette and a Captain Jepson discussed conditions in France, her hatred of the Nazis and her sympathy for ordinary Germans, caught up in the horror of Hitler's ambitions. Then came the bombshell. He asked her to volunteer to work as a special agent. 'You could be of great value to us. We need people who know and love France, who can move about easily and not be noticed.'

Odette was stunned. She had never considered leaving her children. Jepson reminded her that many women had had no such choice — their children were in concentration camps, or missing, or machine-gunned on French roads. 'But,' said Odette, 'I am just an ordinary woman, a housewife and mother. I don't think I am suitable.'

'I believe you are,' replied Jepson. 'If you agree to come for training, we shall know for certain. It's your decision — we only take volunteers.' After Odette had left to think this over, Jepson wrote on her file, 'Direct-minded and courageous. God help the Nazis if we can get her near enough to them.'

The decision is made
Back home, Odette watched her children playing and wondered where they would be now if she had stayed in France. Would they be in a

A warden takes charge of a child rescued from her home hit by a crashed plane. At first, the rates of compensation to which women in the Civil Defence were entitled were lower than those of men, although the risks they faced were the same.

Refugees: desperation clearly shows in this girl's face. Thousands of families like hers had to leave their bombed-out homes and flee from the advancing German armies.

concentration camp? Would they still be alive? Could she expect other people to safeguard her children's future while she did nothing? She remembered her grandfather's words, 'You will be expected to do your duty just as your father did.' Yet how could she go to the war and leave her children alone? Then came a letter from her mother, lonely and despairing in France. Odette knew then that she could not live with herself unless she tried to do something. She comforted herself with the thought that she was bound to fail the training course and could come back to her children with a clear conscience, knowing she had tried her best. Her mind at peace at last, Odette volunteered.

She was quickly enrolled into the First Aid Nursing Yeomanry (FANY), the usual 'cover' for women agents. She found a boarding school for

We were vitally concerned with essential guts. We wanted people who could obey instructions blindly but intelligently, people inspired with confidence and passionate belief, people who would carry on however hopeless perseverance seemed to be.

Maurice Buckmaster,
Specially Employed

the children and an aunt to look after them in the holidays. She told everyone she was being posted to Scotland. Since December 1941, unmarried women between the ages of twenty-five and thirty were subject to call up, with a choice between industry or the services. Odette seemed just like another woman in uniform. Leaving her children for the first time in their lives, Odette joined a handful of other women in a country house, where she spoke only French and was known by her code name, CÉLINE.

Women spies

Up to the twentieth century, the more usual image of female intelligence agents was that of the 'femme fatale' who used her beauty, sex and intelligence to obtain information by deceiving her victims. The First World War saw a change of style and a new professionalism in order to equip agents for dangerous work in enemy-occupied territory. Women made an important contribution in this less glamorous but crucial role. But it was the formation of SOE in the Second World War which created the most equal opportunities for men and women in intelligence work. Women were selected not for sexual attractiveness but on the same basis as men: for their ability to master languages and wireless operations, to operate in lonely, dangerous conditions and to work effectively with local resistance groups. Their training and tasks were as arduous and demanding as those of the men.

Women are frequently very skilful at eliciting information; they require no disguise; if attractive they are likely to be welcome everywhere, and may be able to seduce from their loyalty those whose assistance or indiscretion may be of use. On the other hand, they are variable . . . and apt to be reckless. Their treatment requires the most watchful discretion.

Colonel David Henderson, first British intelligence manual, 1904

This photograph is taken from Now It Can Be Told, *a film about life in the SOE made after the war. It shows an agent practising to blow up a train. Women were taught the same sabotage techniques as men and the key role of the SOE during the Allied invasion would be to help the resistance fighters cut vital German communication lines.*

Odette spent her days learning self-defence, morse code, map reading, and how to fire a gun and poach for food. She learnt about conditions in occupied France, how to avoid being caught, and what to do if she was arrested. Nothing in her sheltered life had prepared Odette for this, but she was determined to do her best and complete the course, even if she was turned down at the end. She proved adaptable and got on well with people. Recruits came from all walks of life. They had many reasons for volunteering — ranging from patriotism to a simple thirst for adventure. The most reliable proved to be those who saw this as their best contribution to winning the war.

The final report on Odette was mixed — and not unlike her school report of thirteen years ago:

> 'CÉLINE has enthusiasm and seems to have absorbed the teaching ... She is, however, impulsive and hasty in her judgements ... She is excitable and temperamental although she has a certain determination ... Her main asset is her patriotism ... Her main weakness is her complete unwillingness to admit she could ever be wrong.'

This wasn't really good enough for an agent whose life, and the lives of others, might depend on balanced judgement. But Maurice Buckmaster, head of one of SOE's French sections, saw her stubbornness as an important asset. He decided to trust his instinct and took her on. Odette, who had expected to fail and go home happily, now realised that she had wanted to succeed all along.

Preparation for France

Odette went through the final stages of training to make her part of a team. These usually consisted of an organiser, a radio operator and a courier. In wartime Europe, an able-bodied man moving round delivering messages or money was too conspicuous. Women could pass unnoticed and travel almost everywhere. They were very much in demand as couriers. Women were also often trained as radio operators, the most dangerous job of all, since the Germans could tune into a transmission and arrest an operator red-handed.

Odette was briefed in minute detail about daily life in France. This information, culled from radio, newspaper and agents' reports, covered everything from the latest fashions to the use of ration cards. Her clothes needed French labels, and her teeth French fillings. One false detail could arouse suspicion and result in arrest.

A still from Now It Can Be Told, *showing a woman agent learning to handle a gun on an SOE training course. Only women from the special services were allowed to carry weapons. Of the 500 SOE agents sent to France, 39 were women.*

Operation 'Clothier'

Odette's job was to organise a new network at Auxerre, in the German occupied zone. She agreed on condition that she could choose a local man as leader. 'I will liaise with London, but he will be more acceptable to the local resistance than a young woman fresh from England,' she explained. Her code name in the field was to be LISE. Odette Sansom, British housewife and mother of three, no longer existed. She was Odette Metayer, a widow with no children. Even her own wedding ring had been filed off and replaced. She knew it would be hard to live this fiction for months on end, but her life depended on it.

Odette memorised her instructions:

OPERATION 'CLOTHIER' —

Code name: LISE. **Destination:** Auxerre.
To be received by RAOUL in Cannes. To cross demarcation line to Auxerre. To get established and obtain details of WT operator in Paris for communicating with London.
Mission: To find a 'safe' house for agents and escapers. To recruit local members to the circuit and supply information.
Password: 'Connaissez-vous un bon coiffeur par ici?'
(Do you know of a good hairdresser round here?)
Reply: 'Cela dépend de ce que vous voulez dire par bon.'
(That all depends on what you mean by good.)

In September, Odette said goodbye to her children as cheerfully as she could, and wrote a great bundle of letters, for the SOE to post at intervals. Buckmaster gave her a farewell present — a silver powder compact — and another less welcome 'gift' — a poison pill which, in the last resort, would kill her in six seconds. Dressed in French

Throughout the [Second World] War, women in many countries were employed in every branch of intelligence . . . They were collectors, collators, analysts, evaluators, interpreters and couriers . . . They were ubiquitous and invaluable.

Jock Haswell,
Spies and Spymasters

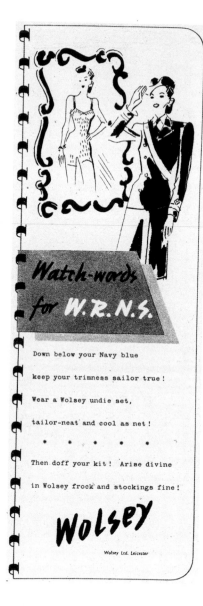

clothes from head to toe, and clutching a bunch of violets for luck, she set off to fly to Gibraltar.

Leaving, however, was not so easy. Indeed, it became almost a joke. The first attempt failed when another plane crashed into hers before take-off. The second was cancelled when the French due to receive her were arrested by the Gestapo. A seaplane journey was put off by bad weather. Her next try was nearly fatal — her plane crashed on take-off, and finished up on the edge of a cliff. After each failure, the SOE would laugh and tell her she was getting very expensive. 'Sorry about that,' she said, 'two aircraft gone, my hat gone, but I did save the violets.'

Finally, Odette embarked on a troopship to Gibraltar, from where she was to sail to France. However, she had a battle to get the Polish captain of the sailing boat to take her. It was a stormy voyage in every way. He showed her a mountain of dirty crockery and shouted, 'You're a woman — so get on with it.' She did, with bucket after bucket of cold sea water. He drank so heavily that she thought it was dangerous and tossed his whisky bottle overboard. In his fury at this, he threatened to throttle her. Odette was glad to reach land. As she stepped ashore, she was overwhelmed by the pungent smell of thyme and sage in the warm Mediterranean night. 'That smell of herbs still carries me back vividly to that moment of landing.' Unmistakably — she was back in France.

Chapter Five

In the Field

When Odette landed, in November 1942, southern France was still controlled by the collaborationist Vichy government of Marshal Pétain. (The rest of the country was under German occupation.) She was taken straight to Cannes and to RAOUL, whose real name was Peter Churchill. Odette, eager and impatient as ever, was anxious to get to Auxerre and begin her job. Where were the papers she needed to cross into occupied territory? After a day or two, bored with waiting, she asked for something to do. Peter Churchill sent her off on a tough first assignment. She had to escort two male agents to Marseilles, hand over 200,000 francs hidden in a newspaper to an agent in a café, and collect a vital suitcase. The suitcase contained plans of the Marseilles docks, invaluable information for the Allies which they would use when planning their invasion of occupied France.

France, 1942

▼ *Vichy police and German soldiers check a woman's identity papers.*

It was an exhilarating experience for her to be at liberty in France, among her own people. Odette completed her mission but missed the last train home. The only available bed was in a brothel used by German soldiers, where the manageress was a patriotic Frenchwoman. As luck would have it, German military police raided the brothel that night, looking for deserters. The manageress saved Odette by saying she was her niece, highly infectious with scarlet fever.

On her return to Cannes, there was still no sign

These propaganda posters put up by the Germans to allay the fears of returning French refugees read: 'Abandoned Populations — Have faith in the German soldiers.'

of her papers. In the days of waiting, she delivered more money and messages. She liaised with local resistance. She found 'safe' houses for the team's radio operator ARNAUD, and looked for fields suitable for landing the Lysander aircraft which brought in vital mail and new agents. Once she crossed into occupied France and travelled to Paris, a difficult and dangerous journey. Odette proved to be good at this risky work, quick-thinking and cool-headed.

Peter Churchill found her increasingly useful, but Odette hated Cannes. She felt she had not made the painful decision to leave her children and come to France in order to watch sleek collaborators working with the Germans and being as friendly with them as if the war had never happened. She wanted to be in the thick of the fight in the occupied zone.

However, the fortunes of war were changing fast. On 11 November, ten days after Odette's arrival, German armies invaded Vichy France, and she no longer needed to go to Auxerre to fight the enemy. She, Peter and ARNAUD made a good team and Peter radioed London saying LISE was 'indispensable'.

Odette admired Peter's dedication, and although she found ARNAUD difficult and hot-tempered, she knew he was an excellent radio operator. The team achieved success against great odds. Their main problem was jealousy between local groups, especially over equipment dropped by British planes. Odette soon found out that an agent's life consisted mostly of long, dreary stretches of boredom and loneliness, punctuated by short bursts of action, danger and exhilaration. What kept her going was that she was now caught up in the war. The cost of defeat was all too obvious — she was surrounded by people who had suffered in some way. Some were refugees. Many had relatives in camps, on forced labour teams or killed in action.

ARNAUD, Captain A. Rabinovich, was captured by the Gestapo and executed in 1944.

Danger and disappointment

Sometimes there were mistakes. On Odette's first night operation, when a Hudson bomber was due to pick up five important French generals, the leader of the local resistance had chosen an impossible field for the landing. They watched helplessly as the Hudson circled then, receiving no signal, climbed again and set off back to England.

There was extreme danger too. Once they were ambushed at a disused airfield while waiting for a Lysander pick-up. They scattered in different directions to escape. Odette was pursued by a tracker dog — one of her worst childhood nightmares. She plunged into an icy river to make the dog lose her scent. It worked, but she could not return to town till curfew ended in the morning. Then, freezing cold, she tramped the ten kilometres back. 'I decided to brazen it out by sitting in full view on a café terrace hoping the others would find me. At the next table four Germans were saying how easy it would be to catch the fugitives!'

After this incident, the group returned to Cannes but their cover was already blown. The Gestapo had rounded up most of Peter's network and raided his flat. Odette was not yet a suspect so, while Peter stayed in hiding, she had the difficult job of tying up loose ends, and fixing new identity cards. Peter Churchill said later that the three months in which she had been his courier had given him every opportunity to judge her worth. He left much tricky work to her. She never complained and he had total confidence in her. He recognised in her someone whose spirit, sense of humour and lively nature stubbornly refused to be dominated by defeat or to be afraid of German soldiers.

Her name was LISE and from her . . . there emanated a distinct aura of challenge that was only intensified by the determined set of her chin . . . A fearless look suggested that not even the thought of the prisons held any terrors for this girl.

Peter Churchill, Duel of Wits

To get a better idea of the *'terrible hold'* the Germans had taken on the capital I begged a friend to take me to lunch at Maxims. Gathered there were the Nazi intelligentsia and the pretty little *'grey mice'* escorted by dashing Luftwaffe officers ... They were being served with delicate and delicious foods, and I thought of my poor devils travelling the length and breadth of France on empty bellies, down at heel, yet working to get rid of all this arrogant lot and their collaborators with them.

Marie Madeleine Fourcade,
Noah's Ark

A French resistance fighter,
probably from Paris. The
'maquisards' operated in the south
where they could hide in the low
scrubland called 'maquis'.

Chapter Six

Betrayal

In February 1943, Odette and Peter arrived at their new base in St Jorioz, a small village in the French Alps a few miles from Annecy. They found rooms in the main hotel and a remote hut for Arnaud and his radio.

Then came a stroke of luck. Jean Cottet at the hotel put them in touch with the leader of the local maquis, Captain Tom Morel. He commanded a large force, mostly of young men avoiding forced labour, from a hideout on the nearby Plateau de Glières. Arnaud radioed London at once.

> 'Most urgent. 2000 determined well-officered maquisards stationed Annecy expecting attack . . . Urge you arm these men soonest . . . Incentive to other maquis through their victory incalculable.'

Back came the reply:

> 'Well done. This is what we have been waiting for. Warn maquisards prepare three large bonfires at 100 yard intervals . . . Light only at sound of squadron approach. Expect 126 containers midnight — 2 am, March 13. Rain, hail or flak . . . Tallyho.'

Before the drop took place, Peter was recalled to London. Odette now took full responsibility for the circuit. 'In Jorioz, I really felt I was achieving something at last, especially acting as the link with Morel during the arms drop.' Months later, about 450 men, led by Morel, used the arms to successfully resist attack by 10,000 Germans who had surrounded the plateau. The maquis killed 300 Germans for the loss of only twelve Frenchmen.

You were stuck in a room — just four walls with nothing of your own and nothing to do but wait for the next call. It's a lonely job and you can't talk to anyone about it — not even the people you are closest to. It's hard to develop a relationship with people when you can't say anything about your life in England.

Odette

Maquisards operating a radio in the snow. One stands guard while the other transmits. Most messages to headquarters were in morse code but SOE London used the BBC's Foreign Service to send coded instructions to agents in the field.

Bardet: Double Agent

Odette had recently been introduced to a new member of the network. Roger Bardet had supposedly made a miraculous escape from a German prison and was now assistant to Marsac, leader of the Marseilles circuit. 'I don't trust him. He's got fishy eyes,' Odette warned, but the others laughed at what they called feminine intuition.

Odette was right. Bardet was a double agent in the pay of the German Military Intelligence — the Abwehr. He soon secretly betrayed Marsac, who was then approached in prison by Hugo Bleicher, of the Abwehr. Bleicher's story was that,

DES LIBÉRATEURS?

GRZYWACZ
JUIF POLONAIS
2 ATTENTATS

ELEK
JUIF HONGROIS
8 DÉRAILLEMENTS

WASJBROT
JUIF POLONAIS
1 ATTENTAT · 5 DÉRAILLEMENTS

WITCHITZ
JUIF POLONAIS
15 ATTENTATS

FINGERWEIG
JUIF POLONAIS
3 ATTENTATS · 6 DÉRAILLEMENTS

BOCZOV
JUIF HONGROIS
CHEF DÉRAILLEUR
20 ATTENTATS

FONTANOT
COMMUNISTE ITALIEN
12 ATTENTATS

MANOUCHIAN
ARMÉNIEN
CHEF DE BANDE
56
ATTENTATS
150 MORTS
600 BLESSÉS

RAYMAN
JUIF POLONAIS
13 ATTENTATS

ALFONSO
ESPAGNOL ROUGE
7 ATTENTATS

LA LIBÉRATION!
PAR L'ARMÉE DU CRIME

A German propaganda poster blaming acts of resiştance and sabotage on foreigners, Jews and Communists. Its overall message to the French population is that members of the resistance are terrorists and criminals, not freedom fighters.

although German, he hated the Nazis. He needed to contact the Jorioz circuit to get himself to England where he wanted to discuss plans with the British authorities for ending the war. Marsac chose to believe this tale and gave Bleicher all the names he wanted, including Odette's.

The net was tightening. Bleicher visited Annecy, found Odette and told her the same unlikely story. 'I took it with a heavy pinch of salt,' she remembers

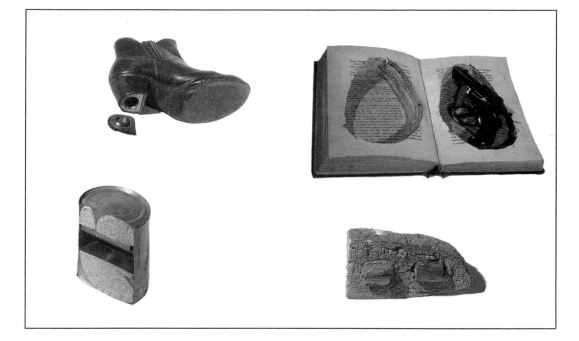

but, desperately playing for time, she outwardly agreed to his suggestions. Yes, she would contact London and ask for an aircraft to pick him up. But she warned him that this could not be before the next full moon, on 18 April. Odette now worked fast. A report was immediately radioed to London. ROGER, a newly-arrived British agent, was sent away and everyone else in the Annecy area warned to keep clear. Soon she heard from London that Peter was to return by parachute on 15 April. She chose a suitable landing site 2000 metres up the Semnoz mountain. Now all she could do was pray that he would arrive safely so that they could 'disappear' before Bleicher's return on the 18th.

As soon as they heard the BBC radio announcer begin the coded message confirming Peter's return, Odette, ARNAUD and Jean Cottet started struggling up the mountainside in the dark and the snow. Peter made a perfect landing. They hid the arms and equipment which had floated down with him and returned to their base.

Secret documents and equipment used by the resistance were sometimes concealed in the most ingenious places.

Intelligence is not, nor can it ever be, an exact science. Time and time again the fate of a spy has depended on some chance, incident or coincidence which could not possibly have been foreseen.

Jock Haswell,
Spies and Spymasters

37

Next day, Odette travelled to Annecy to alert Morel about the hidden arms and to organise her departure with Peter the following morning. But she did not know that Bardet had passed on this information to Bleicher. Nor did she suspect that the Abwehr were also learning a great deal from another informant within SOE's London headquarters.

Capture

In the middle of that night, Jean Cottet knocked on Odette's door, saying an agent wanted to see her urgently. She walked downstairs to find Bleicher's cool gaze and three guns trained on her. It was over. There was nothing to do but remain silent and hope that ARNAUD and the others had

Resistance fighters are led away under arrest by the Milice, a French security force working alongside the Germans. They faced torture and execution.

got away. Odette was hustled upstairs to watch Peter being roughly shaken awake and handcuffed. She caught sight of his wallet, which contained vital new radio codes and lists of names. In the confusion, she managed to hide it in her clothes and when they were driven away, she pushed it down the car seat. With luck, it wouldn't be found until it no longer mattered and so give other agents breathing space to cover their tracks.

Peter was badly affected by imprisonment and soon tried to escape. He failed and was beaten up. To protect him, Odette told their captors that he was a member of the Churchill family, and that she was his wife. She hoped that they would treat him better if they thought he was a relation of Winston Churchill, the British Prime Minister.

Odette was a tower of strength from the beginning of their captivity, Peter recalled later:

'It seemed right that she should have two names, for here was a girl quite different from the one I had known in the Resistance. [LISE] had proved to be a carefree courier who, whilst capable of taking important decisions and able to march with the best, never really took the thing seriously. . . . Odette was a person facing a situation that required moral fibre and in this lonely contest she had clearly revealed herself as a winner.'

Before long they were handed over to the Gestapo at Toulon. Some days later, they were taken to Paris, and by armed guard to the notorious Fresnes prison.

In the end a spy is nearly always on his or her own in a lonely, dangerous world, where survival and success may depend entirely on exploiting a sudden opportunity with courage and swiftness of reaction.

Jock Haswell,
Spies and Spymasters

This new fear and the feeling of helplessness, was something which my imagination had never foreseen except in nightmares.

Peter Churchill, describing imprisonment in
The Spirit of the Cage

Chapter Seven

Imprisonment and Torture

Inside Fresnes, Odette was roughly strip-searched by a grim wardress. Then, wearing her own clothes, she was marched to cell No 108. The sign on the door read, 'No concessions of any kind'. She was pushed in and the door slammed shut.

The cell, four by three metres, contained a rusty bed, a broken chair, a lavatory, a cold water tap and a basin, tin bowl and spoon. It was 8 May 1943. Here she would spend the next seven months in solitary confinement. The terrible process of trying to make her less than human had begun. Odette recognised that to resist this would be far harder than anything she had done as a secret agent. She knew that to survive she must never let her jailers or the hardships of prison overwhelm her. She was determined to assert her independence from the outset.

Solitary confinement can break the human spirit. To fight this Odette searched for ways, however small, of keeping in touch with the outside world. She began by smashing a pane in her nailed-up cell window with the broken chair. The punishment was three days without food, but it was worth it just to see the clouds idling across the sky. She found ways of talking to other prisoners. 'High up in one corner of my cell was a central heating grill. By standing on a chair, you could talk down to the person in the cell below.' This was Michelle, in prison for her Communist beliefs. They became friends and also learnt to communicate by tapping on the walls. Odette became part of the support network which united all the women. They were hungry for news. She passed on what she had learnt from Peter: German forces were being

In solitary confinement twenty-four hours are endless — sometimes I felt there was no difference between twenty-four hours and twenty-four months. The only way to escape is with your mind. After all, no one can control our minds if we don't want them to.

Odette

Anna Neagle took the lead role in the film Odette. *It was partly shot on location at Fresnes, where Odette had been one of 3,000 prisoners held by the Gestapo. Odette acted as an advisor to the film and was present during the shooting, reliving some of the experiences she wished to forget.*

expelled from North Africa, the Russians were forcing them back on the Eastern Front, and Germany itself was being heavily bombed.

Survival mechanisms

Odette forced herself to live each minute as it came. She crossed off each day on a makeshift calendar, scratched on the grimy wall with a hairgrip. The days themselves were measured by the prison routine: the noisy round of the food trolley, the harsh shouted orders of the guards to the prisoners leaving their cells for the exercise yard — or for the execution yard, she never knew which.

The hard and lonely lessons learnt during her childhood illnesses came back to her. She remembered how to leave her body and her surroundings behind and escape into her mind. She lay on the hard straw mattress, firmly shutting out the screams of the prisoners and the shouts of the guards, and filling her mind with the stories and poems she had learnt from her grandfather. She made up new songs to the music of her childhood.

Sundays were the worst. The prison was as still as a tomb. Those who killed themselves in despair always did it on a Sunday.

Odette

In her mind's eye, she redecorated and refurbished every room in every house she had ever known. These images became so real to her that when she went home after the war, it was a shock to see that the curtains were the 'wrong' colour. Odette thought constantly of her children, especially at night. She summoned up pictures of them against the darkness — playing out of doors, setting off to school or tucked up in bed. She talked to them and heard their voices.

The Gestapo's orders were that Odette 'Churchill' must be kept apart from the others. In the whole seven months, she had no exercise, no showers, no chance even to wash her hair. Throughout her imprisonment, she wore the dark grey flannel suit she had chosen in London for its good quality material. Every day she moved the skirt round an inch to prevent it wearing. Such attention to detail was typical of Odette and her strategies for survival. She established small but significant routines, to give shape to otherwise blank and endless days.

Her craving for food grew stronger daily. The allotted two cups of coffee and bowl of soup with black bread was never enough. But worse still was the hunger for human contact and affection. Each visit from the German chaplain was an oasis in a desert of isolation. He passed on messages to Peter, who remembered him afterwards as 'the first person to speak to me like a human being'.

Odette's only other visitor was Hugo Bleicher, the Abwehr officer who had arrested her. He often tried to persuade her to save herself from the Gestapo by co-operating with him. She flatly rejected his offers of better treatment, books, even a visit to Paris, in return for information. She laughed at the idea that she might turn traitor. He told her the name of the informant who he said was working for Germany inside SOE, knowing she could do nothing to prevent further betrayal of her colleagues. 'I had to live with this knowledge for the next two years, wondering whether the SOE knew about him', she remembers with anguish.

Interrogation and torture

Thirteen times during her year at Fresnes, Odette heard the ominous shout 'Tribunal' outside her cell and was taken to Gestapo headquarters. Peering through the grille of the prison van, she got her first glimpse of the real world since her arrest — a group of children playing in the streets. It reminded her vividly of her own daughters. Odette refused to answer questions and was sent back to her cell.

Three days later, the shout came again. Odette put on her one precious pair of silk stockings to keep her courage up. The interrogator was a fresh-faced young man. He began to question her:

> 'Where is your radio operator, ARNAUD?'
> 'I have nothing to say.'
> 'Where did you send the British agent ROGER?'
> 'I have nothing to say.'
> 'Where are the plans of the Marseilles docks?'
> 'I have nothing to say.'

> 'The SOE had told me what to expect. But the Gestapo made a great mistake — they put me in a chair facing the window. I could see the sky and the trees of the Bois de Boulogne. I thought, if I keep focusing on that, I can get away from all this, because I hadn't seen trees for so long.'

As another man, a Frenchman, twisted her arms behind the chair, her interrogator said, 'I am going to make you answer. I shall unbutton your blouse.' Odette coolly replied, 'I prefer to do that myself.' Then the assistant laid a red hot bar against her spine. Through a haze of pain, she heard the three questions being repeated and forced out the same

If you look into the eyes of the man who is torturing you he knows he cannot win. You are stronger than he is. He can kill you but that is all. Once you feel that your behaviour is quite different.

Odette

Imprisonment and torture is a battle you must fight every day and never expect to win finally. You have to fight each day's battle as it comes. You have to recognise that you may lose the last battle. But you hold on to yourself and to life until it is taken from you.

Odette

reply, 'I have nothing to say.'

'You are very stubborn, Frau Churchill. Now my assistant will pull out your toenails one by one. Each time I shall ask the same questions. If you faint we shall revive you and begin again.' She stared at the trees and the sky, saying to herself, 'the only thing I can and will think about is that I will go on refusing to speak.' The assistant knelt at her feet, took out a pair of pliers and set to work. As each wave of pain receded, she heard the questions and managed to utter the same reply. She clung on desperately to the thought, 'I may lose my body but I don't have to give away my soul.'

Waves of pain came, sank, came again. She could no longer speak, but only shake her head in reply. She could see the blood oozing from her feet, and the Frenchman staring at her. She realised with horror that he did not see her as a human being, just as a pair of feet he was operating on. She stared back. 'After my feet, they were going to start on my hands. I wondered how much more I could take. Then a senior officer came in. "This is useless", he said. "You can kill her but you will not make her talk. Take her back."'

Back in her cell she showed her mutilated feet to the horrified chaplain, but made him promise not to tell Peter. But he did report that 'Odette is behaving with great dignity and has earned the respect of many.'

Condemned to die

Several days later, still unable to walk on her torn and bloody feet, Odette was taken before a Gestapo Court. She was sentenced without trial and condemned on two counts, as a Frenchwoman and as a British spy. 'Even at the worst times there was always a voice inside me saying "Don't take yourself too seriously." So now I thought, this is so German, it is almost funny. I shall never know

Peter Churchill. As a British officer, he was not tortured in the way that Odette was. Peter received several visitors and on one occasion was able to leave the prison with Bleicher to see a friend.

for which country I am dying. "You must take your pick of the counts, gentlemen," I told them, "I can only die once." '

A red cross, meaning 'condemned', was splashed across her cell door. She knew that death might come at any time, yet the days passed and nothing happened. 'Every day that I survived, I tried to prepare myself for the next. I even made hair curlers out of an old stocking so that I could look my best facing the firing squad. I thought: if they come to get me, I will look them in the eye until they shoot me.'

Somehow, having survived torture and everything the Nazis had subjected her to, Odette had achieved a tranquillity which helped her to live with the ever present possibility of death. Nor did she fear any longer that she might be dehumanised by her experience. She saw clearly that it was her torturers who had become less than human.

Chapter Eight

Condemned

When you have been condemned to death it sets your mind free. You are able to take any risk.

Odette

'This is the warmonger Winston Churchill who neither sees the signs of the times nor knows the true voice of his own people.' This German propaganda poster portrays him in much the same light as Hitler was by the British.

The months dragged on, and the Gestapo continued to question her. Odette told them nothing, but made sure that they believed that she and Peter were married and relatives of Winston Churchill. It was also not too difficult to convince them that Peter was less important in the Resistance, and was in France mainly because of her. After all, he had arrived from England only a day before their arrest and she had been in charge of the St Jorioz circuit at the time. Indeed, the Germans were sufficiently convinced to consider releasing Peter in exchange for a senior German officer. They regarded Odette as the key prisoner; her refusal to speak under torture confirmed this view. Her French nationality also counted heavily against her.

Despite the daily cruelties and indignities inflicted by some of the prison staff, Odette felt no anger or bitterness. 'I kept thinking, I am not one of you. No matter what you do to me I shall never become one of you. That is what saved me.' When one wardress hit her for no reason, Odette demanded to see the prison captain to complain. He was a retired soldier, trying to do an unpleasant job as best he could. Like the chaplain, he was out of sympathy with the Nazis, and was impressed by her dignity and personality.

In October, weakened by cold weather, confinement and poor food, Odette caught pneumonia. Without informing the Gestapo, the prison captain ordered her removal to better quarters. Odette refused this favour. With her own brand of faith, she had come to feel that by willingly accepting her sufferings she was bearing a small share of all human suffering. Perhaps because of her childhood illnesses, she felt better fitted to shoulder this burden than many others.

Recovery

At last, when she was too ill to protest, Odette was moved to a lighter, warmer cell with three other women. One, an invalid, was allowed extra food parcels which Odette shared. 'This food, and the human contact, probably saved my life.' There was even food to spare for Peter, which a wardress smuggled to him. By now, the balance of war so clearly favoured the Allies that it seems that some prison staff thought it useful to curry favour with a 'Churchill'.

Odette's recovery was slow. The captain arranged for her to work in the sewing room, where conditions were easier and where German uniforms were made and repaired. She stubbornly refused, saying, 'I am a political prisoner and I refuse to do anything to help the German war effort.' She chose instead to make two dolls — a Christmas present for the chaplain's niece and nephew. She continued to make demands of her captors because 'it proves to other people that you still exist and must be reckoned with'. Her blouse was spotted with blood from the torture. She gave it to Bleicher demanding to have it cleaned.

One day she was sent to have her fingerprints taken. With joy, she picked out Peter in the crowd of prisoners. It was wonderful to have this chance to talk. Everyone had heard on the prison grapevine that the Allies were winning. British and American troops had landed in Italy to expel the Germans. An invasion of France could not be far off. They knew the fingerprinting meant they would be leaving Fresnes, probably for Germany. Odette feared the Nazis would find it easier to dispose of her quietly there. Even so, Peter remembered 'her morale was sky high, where she

The dolls Odette made for the prison chaplain's niece and nephew from bits of old underwear, bedding straw, scraps of wool and tiny pieces of material. Several years after the war the chaplain's nephew came to England. Thinking Odette was dead, the chaplain had sent back the dolls to be passed on to her children.

had put it through her own optimistic personality — it imposed itself on other prisoners and guards alike!' Peter was not under sentence of death so, with luck, he might now be sent to a reasonable camp and survive the war. On Valentine's Day 1944, she heard he had gone to Berlin.

The human spirit

By April, Odette had been in prison for almost a year. In spite of the evil she had experienced, she had come to feel that there was a force of goodness which was stronger and which could not be extinguished. 'In Fresnes I knew of wonderful people who were an example to everyone because of their courage. The endurance and courage of so many other prisoners seemed to reach through the thick walls and tiny windows into my cell.'

Sometimes, steeled to expect the worst, she was amazed at the extraordinary things which happened. One day she told the guard it was her

French resistance fighters showing the Allies the exact location of German defences near Cherbourg in June 1944. The Allied invasion of France was the goal towards which Odette and other agents had been working.

WOMEN AGENTS WHO DIED IN CONCENTRATION CAMPS

NATZWEILER	DACHAU	RAVENSBRÜCK
Vera Leigh (d. July 1944)	Noor Inayat Khan (d. September 1944)	Denise Bloch (d. February 1944)
Diana Rowden (d. July 1944)	Yolande Beeckman (d. September 1944)	Violette Szabo (d. February 1944)
Andrée Borrel (d. July 1944)	Eliane Plewman (d. September 1944)	Lilian Rolfe (d. February 1944)
Sonia Oschanesky (d. July 1944)	Madeleine Demerment (d. September 1944)	Cecily LeFort (d. early 1945)
		Yvonne Rudillat (d. April 1945)

birthday. 'What would you like?' he asked. Tired of the continual harsh shouts of the guards, she said, 'To hear a beautiful voice.' An hour later, she was astonished to hear a wonderful voice singing outside her cell. The guard had found a prisoner who was a famous singer in Paris and ordered him to perform for her birthday. Most of the prison staff were thoroughly brutalised by their work but such rare signs of humanity, rising above the misery and degradation of prison life, helped Odette and others to keep going.

Early in May, Odette made her last journey to Gestapo Headquarters. After one year and four days, she was leaving Fresnes for good. On arrival, she found six other women, all SOE agents also on their way to Germany. They were delighted to see one another and to exchange experiences. Later the women were handcuffed and taken by train to Karlsrühe prison. Odette never saw any of them again. She was the only one condemned to death, yet the only one to survive. Three were killed at Dachau concentration camp and the others died in the Natzweiler prison.

Noor Inayat Khan, MADELEINE, arrived in France by Lysander in June 1943 and worked as a radio operator in Paris until her arrest by the Gestapo. She was executed at Dachau in September 1944.

Chapter Nine

Cheating Death

I prayed, not kneeling down, but all the time, as though suffering was a prayer. I thought, I can't ask for a miracle. I don't deserve one. Perhaps my experiences are not wasted if I am sharing in the world's suffering, rather than being one of those who are inflicting pain . . . I was convinced that every experience I had ever had had been a preparation.

Odette

Odette spent eight weeks in Karlsrühe prison, during which the long-awaited invasion began. On 6 June 1944, Allied troops landed in Normandy and the Resistance were able to fight openly at last. No doubt because of the Allied advance, Odette was moved deeper into Germany, to Frankfurt. Here prisoners were locked into cages in a huge room, where harsh lights were kept permanently on. 'There was no privacy, asleep or awake. We were always on show, like animals behind bars.'

Soon she was on the move again, this time by cattle truck to Halle, where she shared an attic room with a huddled, despairing mass of women from the Ukraine. The smell and filth were indescribable. Once, Odette heard her name called. A German soldier stood in the doorway.

'Are you Frau Churchill?'

'Yes.'

He punched her brutally in the mouth. 'Take that for Winston Churchill from me.'

Somehow Odette managed to keep her courage up throughout these endless, apparently pointless journeys. Why did they have to move her around like this, just in order to execute her? She longed to stay still in a properly organised camp. When, on the move again, eighty kilometres north of Berlin, she saw the buildings of Ravensbrück, she thought, 'I am in luck at last.' How wrong she was.

Concentration Camp

Passing between rows of huts, where starved, shaven-headed inmates stared and shouted, she was taken to a shower room and locked in for the

night. Next morning, Odette appeared before the camp commandant Fritz Sühren. He was icily polite and told her she would be placed in the bunker (the camp prison) with 'punishment' food rations, no books, exercise or showers. She took a last look at the sky and a deep breath of fresh air, before she was marched down and locked into the stale blackness of the underground cell. Solitary confinement here was far worse than at Fresnes. There was no cell window to break, no Michelle to talk to, no interviews with Bleicher, just months of solitary misery.

She learnt to separate day and night by the arrival of food and the regular screaming of the women who were beaten every evening in the

There are moments when there comes to you, through your own suffering, a consciousness of the suffering of the whole world. It is only these moments which make it possible to go on.

Concentration camp survivor

51

punishment cell next door. Once a month, the darkness was split by light, as the cell door was flung open and Fritz Sühren stood in the doorway. 'Have you anything to say?'

'No.'

Then the door slammed and pitch darkness enveloped her again.

Odette remained in her black, silent cell for three months and eleven days. Just as she had done at Fresnes, she travelled back to the stories and poems of her childhood. Her experience of blindness helped her to live an inner life of the mind. Stretched out on the hard bed, twenty-four hours a day, she called up her own worlds of colour, movement and sound. To fill the heavy hours, she decided to make clothes for her children. In her imagination, she measured them, chose the material, designed, cut and stitched the clothes and dressed the girls in them.

Amongst us all, however, the living and the dead, there existed a fraternity stronger than anything on earth; it was as if we belonged to an immense community, outside the human race, situated on a mysterious planet, where the macabre, the ridiculous, the grotesque rubbed shoulders and intermingled in a fantastic and irrational chaos.

Denise Du-fournier, Ravensbrück 1948

The Allied advance, August 1944.

The Allies advance

In August, Allied armies landed in southern France, where Odette had worked. It was decided she must be punished for her part in equipping the Resistance there. The central heating in her cell was turned up, the air supply blocked and she was starved for a week. The heat was unbearable. 'I wrapped myself in a wet blanket. It got so painful, I could feel my stomach sticking to my spine. I soon got so weak, I knew I could not last much longer.' But the Gestapo did not want Odette to die just yet. The prospect of defeat made prisoners like Frau Churchill valuable as possible bargaining tools. A large plateful of food appeared. 'In my state, I could not even touch it. It seemed too good to be true and I thought it must have come from the devil.'

Too weak to stand, racked with fever, dysentery and scurvy, Odette was taken to the camp hospital. She was told she had tuberculosis but was given no treatment. She was, however, moved to a cell above ground. Crossing the prison yard, she had managed to pick up a leaf blown in from the outside. The only beautiful thing in Ravensbrück, it became a precious symbol of the free world beyond the camp. As she lay holding it, all she could hear from her bed were the sounds of the daily roll call to divide the women into work squads and the rumble of the cart, taking last night's dead to the crematorium for burning.

As the Allied armies closed in towards Ravensbrück, conditions in the camp grew worse. Rations were cut again and again, and any prisoners too weak to work were executed. In mid-April 1945, orders came from Berlin that all bunker prisoners be executed — so that no witnesses to the appalling conditions would survive. But, perhaps as a personal insurance policy, Sühren left seven alive, including Odette. At 6 am on her birthday, 28 April, Odette was taken from her cell, put into a luxurious Mercedes with Sühren and driven out of the camp. At the gate she saw guards, soldiers and staff panicking in their attempt to escape from the advancing Russian army. A wardress — one of the cruellest — begged with tears for help, 'Save me, I have three children.' Odette looked at her. 'So have I,' she said flatly.

Freedom
They arrived in another camp, at Neustadt. Here, too, chaos was spreading. When hundreds of prisoners struggled hysterically to get out, the panicky guards mowed them down with machine guns. 'On 3 May,' Odette remembers, 'Sühren came to me to announce Hitler's death — but I was past caring.' Next day, Sühren announced he was handing her over to the Americans. He drove her,

When I first saw daylight after months of darkness it was an extraordinary feeling. I felt I was almost literally drinking the air and swallowing it down. It was almost painful and I could not face the light at first.

Odette

Fritz Sühren, camp commandant at Ravensbrück.

54

Crematorium ovens at Auschwitz concentration camp viewed by visitors after the war.

Because I was so ill they left my fan light open and the cinders floated onto my bed. Towards the end I could hear the screams of the women forced into the crematorium.

Odette

with an escort of SS vehicles, to a village occupied by the US army where he delivered her to the soldiers. Their roles were now reversed: Odette asked for Sühren's gun and briefcase and stated, 'This is Fritz Sühren, the Commandant of Ravensbrück. Please make him your prisoner.'

'That first night of my release was unforgettable. It was a glorious night, full of stars and very cold. The Americans wanted to find me a bed for the night but I preferred to sit in the car. It was so long since I had seen the night sky.'

After nearly two years of imprisonment, Odette needed those solitary hours to bridge the gap between the two worlds of captivity and freedom. 'I felt a mixture of great joy and all kinds of other emotions. It was impossible for me to live as I had done and jump back to normality in a single leap.'

Odette was soon flown home to England. She arrived to find London streets bedecked with flags for the victory celebrations. She still had with her Sühren's gun and his briefcase, containing some clothes, documents and photographs which later helped to identify war criminals. Two days later Peter arrived.

Chapter Ten

A Normal Life

Back in England, Odette found that she had lost all her belongings when her aunt's house had been bombed. Apart from Sühren's pyjamas (which she had to sleep in on the first night), she had two 'souvenirs' — one of her toenails in a little box and the grey suit she had worn throughout her imprisonment. Her health had been shattered. She was awarded a full disability pension and the doctors thought she would live only a few months. The resilience she had shown in prison helped her pull through, but it was three years before her mutilated feet recovered.

Transition

Many people had to make a difficult transition after the war. Once the victory celebrations were over, peacetime often seemed flat, drab and disappointing. As Britain slowly picked up the pieces after years of war, there were shortages of food, clothing, furniture and housing. Servicemen and women waited impatiently for demobilisation but when they got home, they often missed the companionship, the excitement and the organised life of the forces.

Returning servicemen were entitled to have their previous jobs back and though this was generally thought fair, women who had done those jobs well often found it hard to give them up. They found, too, that certain kinds of work were again closed to them — in banks, in engineering, on the railways and the buses. There was resistance, especially by the trade unions and many other people, to the idea of women 'taking jobs from men'. This applied particularly to married women

What is the quality of war that so many miss and which makes peace seem dull, undirectional, lacking in zest ... It was edge, a full awakening ... a heightening caused by fatigue and a sense of danger that made most of the young who could bear the extension of awareness miss forever that singing of the warning senses, that cat awareness. In peacetime, it has to be developed individually, not in the dangerous shortcut imposition of circumstances war provides.

Mary Lee Settle,
All the Brave Promises

Daily Mirror

(MAY 8)

Tuesday, May 8, 1945
No. 12,911   ONE PENNY
Registered at G.P.O. as a Newspaper.

VE-DAY!

PUBLIC HOLIDAY TODAY AND TOMORROW—OFFICIAL

Czechs flown from Britain to save Prague

Soon after a Czech Spitfire squadron left Britain for Czechoslovakia yesterday large formations carrying Czechoslovak ground troops also took off for home—and the battle for the liberation of Prague. The commander, before leaving, said, " This is the greatest day of my life."

IN a final burst of fiendishness, S.S. troops in Prague last night were firing the last shots of the war on helpless Czech civilians.

S.S. men went through the streets driving people out of their homes as other S.S. troops waited to mow them down with machine-guns.

So bad has been the conduct of the German troops that the Wehrmacht commander of the area broadcast a warning to his men to respect international law.

"Some breaches," he actually admitted, had occurred.

But earlier he had announced that he did not recognise what he described as the "armistice."

"German troops will continue to fight until they have secured a free passage out of the country," he added.

According to refugees who have reached Pilsen the S.S. men, knowing that they will be executed when caught, have abandoned all normal conduct.

Another Prague broadcast reached Czechoslovak circles in London yesterday. It was an S O S from the Czechs pleading for speedy Allied help and asking "send us aircraft."

It spoke of heavy fighting in the streets, said the Germans were throwing hand grenades at houses showing Czechoslovak flags and reported the bombing by German planes of broadcasting home and other public buildings.

Meanwhile Patton's famous Fourth Armoured Division is speeding towards the capital and last night was reported to be fifteen miles south of the city.

SPAIN BREAKS WITH GERMANY

Spain has severed diplomatic relations with Germany. It is officially announced in Madrid.

War winners may broadcast today

The Prime Minister will broadcast at 3 p.m. today.

It is probable that later in the afternoon General Eisenhower, Field-Marshal Montgomery and Field-Marshal Alexander will also speak over the radio to the Allied world.

At 9 p.m. the King will broadcast.

Goebbels and his family are found, poisoned

DISCOVERY has been made in Berlin of the bodies of Dr. Goebbels, his wife, and their six children.

They were found by the Russians. All had taken poison and this was the cause of death.

Hitler's body has not been discovered and neither has the body of Goering.

There is now some speculation as to whether, after all, the Fuehrer and Goering may not have fled to a place of hiding.

It is pointed out, however, that their bodies may have been burned and the ashes lost in the wreckage of the burning Chancellery, or some other of Berlin's destroyed buildings.

★On top of the world

★In the heart of London an Allied soldier — he climbed the Eros statue at London's Piccadilly—gets just as high as he can to celebrate the lifting of the shadow from Europe.

Celebrations delay due to a 'technicality'

By BILL GREIG

THIS IS VE-DAY. AFTER FIVE YEARS, EIGHT MONTHS AND FOUR DAYS OF THE BLOODIEST WAR IN HISTORY BRITAIN AND HER ALLIES HAVE GAINED VICTORY IN EUROPE.

Capitulation of Germany to the Allies was announced by Doenitz yesterday—but a mere technicality in the arrangements made with Russia and America delayed the British people's celebration.

One result of the delay is that Britain's workers get two clear days' holiday—today and tomorrow. This Cabinet decision was disclosed last night.

Spend VE in camp, CO's say

"Daily Mirror" Reporter

COMMANDING officers of Army and RAF camps all over Britain told their men yesterday: "Spend VE-Day how you will, but PLEASE spend it in camp."

Thanksgiving services, concerts and later "closing time" for the canteen and sergeants' and officers' mess bars were some of the arrangements to persuade the men to stay in camp.

At an operational station near London the Daily Mirror was told by the Station Commander: "I have a lot of Australian air-crews here and they don't think VE day means the war is over as far as they are concerned. They've volunteered to forgo celebrations to do any odd job that comes up."

German prisoners of war have erected victory flag-poles at Catterick camp in North Yorkshire.

Originally it was intended that the first day's holiday would not begin until the Prime Minister had spoken.

The announcement late last night that today will be VE-Day was the final act in a bewildering day following the German surrender.

The people thronged out into the streets all over the country. In London there were thousands in Whitehall outside Downing-street patiently waiting for the word, little aware of the drama taking place inside No 10

There was chaos and bewilderment where there should have been celebrations.

Here is the story of what happened in No. 10. When the news of the German surrender arrived the Prime Minister was ready to broadcast at 4 p.m. Hurried telephone calls were made to Marshal Stalin and President Truman so that the announcement could be made simultaneously.

Then it was found that the trouble started. It was found that arrangements already made did not allow for the war ending so suddenly.

Mr. Churchill put his broad-

Continued on Back Page

(advertisement partly obscured) ORT YOUR ...INGS

whom the government encouraged to return to their 'traditional' role as home makers.

After the long disruption of war, many women were happy to be able to concentrate on rebuilding a secure family life. But for those who needed or wanted to work, it sometimes seemed that the abilities they had demonstrated during the war had been forgotten. Changes did come, even if they were sometimes slow. By 1947, married women were no longer barred from working in the Civil Service and local government; the teaching, banking and business professions followed suit.

Odette was one of a number of women whose wartime work had broken a different mould. They were in the fighting line, doing the loneliest and riskiest job of all: being a secret agent. They showed that women were quite as capable as men when operating alone in difficult conditions, under constant threat of discovery. They proved to be as professional, resourceful and brave as their male colleagues. But this meant Odette had a much greater transition than most people to make when, after resisting torture and surviving sentence of death, she had to adjust to a normal family existence again. She felt she wanted to bury the last three years in a sealed container and put them behind her, to look forward, never back. It was her children who helped her achieve this. Leaving them had been a heartbreak, but 'coming back closed the wound ... soon, for my children it was as if I had never been away.'

Her marriage to Roy Sansom, however, did not survive their wartime separation. Some time later, Odette married Peter Churchill. 'People saw us as such a romantic couple. It was like a Hollywood film — the story of two secret agents who worked together, were captured and imprisoned, to be finally reunited after the war.' Perhaps, apart from the war, they had little in common and they eventually parted. To Odette, the war had never

I was in the chapel putting the hymn books away. Another girl rushed in saying, 'the headmistress wants you, hurry up and change, then go to the parlour.' I remember we all put on the identical dresses we had made in sewing class. My mother was sitting there wearing a headscarf. There was a split second before we recognised her and one of us rushed forward.

Françoise Miller, remembering her reunion with her mother after the war

been the great adventure some people thought it but simply a necessary job. She wanted to forget, while Peter was one of those who never could do this.

Retribution

She was not allowed to forget for a while. In the winter of 1946, the War Crimes Court at Hamburg were considering events at Ravensbrück. As one of the few survivors, Odette was an important witness. She appeared before the court in FANY uniform, looking very different from the tattered and starving spectre who had escaped from Ravensbrück.

> 'I didn't at all want to relive it or to look for revenge, but I felt I owed it to others. At first I did feel bitterness and anger. No one can go through all that and not feel, "I would like to get my own back". But then you begin to think, what does that make me? It makes me one of them. If I go in that direction it will be like a cancer. I must fight it. I was fortunate because I got over these feelings very quickly. Some of my friends never did.'

What she says echoes the last words of Edith Cavell, before she was shot by the Germans in the First World War. 'Patriotism is not enough. I must have no hatred or bitterness towards anyone.'

Odette also told her story to Jerrard Tickell at the War Office, whose job was to record the experiences of survivors. When it was decided to turn her story into a film, Odette was reluctant. 'There was already quite enough of a Hollywood element in my life without blowing it up into a film.' But she agreed from a sense of responsibility to the families and friends of the dead, for 'it was their story too.'

Odette outside Buckingham Palace with her children in September 1946, after being presented with the George Cross. With them is Captain Peter Churchill who was awarded the DSO.

In 1946, Odette was awarded the George Cross — given only for 'acts of the greatest heroism or of the most conspicuous courage in circumstances of extreme danger.'

An ordinary woman
Until her contact with SOE, Odette had never sought to step out of her domestic role, yet when chance placed her in extraordinary circumstances she displayed qualities which many would regard as 'exceptional'. How did Odette find the strength to survive her ordeal? She was, perhaps, helped a little by luck and by the Churchill name. She herself came to feel she owed much of her courage and faith to the strength of character and ideals of duty instilled in her by her grandfather and her convent education. Her long childhood illness and

blindness, too, had taught her to bear pain, loneliness and darkness without giving in. She knew instinctively that her survival depended on never letting herself be dominated by her captors. Most of us can find hidden reserves of strength and courage at moments of great crisis, but Odette had to call on her reserves day after day — for years — knowing that not once must she slip into despair. She possessed what has been called 'the rarest courage of all — the two o'clock in the morning courage' when the spirit is at its lowest ebb.

Above all, perhaps, her story reminds us that many so-called ordinary people possess exceptional qualities which, through lack of circumstance, lie unrecognised. Several years after the war, Odette wrote her own conclusion:

'I am a very ordinary woman, to whom a chance has been given, to see human beings at their best and at their worst. I knew kindness as well as cruelty, understanding as well as brutality. I completely believe in the potential nobility of the human spirit.'

After her divorce from Peter Churchill, Odette married Geoffrey Hallowes. She has eight grandchildren and is a founder and vice president of the Women of the Year Luncheon.

TIME CHART

Events in Odette's life

1912 28 April – Birth of Odette Marie Céline Brailly, in Amiens, France
1916 Gaston Brailly killed in action
1919 Odette catches polio and suffers temporary blindness
1926 Family move to Boulogne
1931 Odette marries Roy Sansom
1932 Birth of Françoise
1933 Odette and family move to London
1934 Birth of Lili
1936 Birth of Marianne
1939 Roy Sansom called up for active service
1940 Odette moves to Somerset to escape the Blitz
1942 Odette recruited into Special Operations Executive (SOE). November — Odette arrives in Cannes. Joins Peter Churchill's circuit
1943 February — Odette moves with circuit to St Jorioz, near Annecy. March — Peter recalled to London. Marsac betrays circuit to German intelligence. April — Peter returns by parachute. Peter and Odette arrested. May — Odette and Peter taken to Gestapo prison at Fresnes. June — Odette sentenced to death
1944 February — Peter moved from Fresnes to Berlin. May — Odette and six other SOE agents taken to Karlsrühe prison, Germany. July — Odette in solitary confinement in Ravensbrück concentration camp. September — Moved out of solitary confinement
1945 April — Order from Berlin to execute all bunker prisoners; Odette one of seven survivors. May — Odette handed over to American soldiers and flies to England
1946 Odette attends War Crimes court in Hamburg. Receives George Cross
1947 Odette marries Captain Peter Churchill
1950 Odette receives Légion d'Honneur
1956 Odette divorces Peter Churchill and marries Geoffrey Hallowes

Key dates for the Second World War

1914–18 First World War. Ends with Treaty of Versailles

1920 Hitler joins German Workers' Party (later the Nazi Party)

1929 The Great Depression begins

1933 Adolf Hitler becomes German Chancellor

1936 Hitler re-occupies the Rhineland and fortifies it

1938 May — Hitler occupies and annexes Austria. September — The Munich Agreement: Britain and France compel Czechoslovakia to accept Hitler's demands for the Sudetenland

1939 March — Hitler annexes all Czechoslovakia; Britain and France guarantee Poland against attack. 23 August — Germany and USSR sign non-aggression pact. 1 September — Germany invades Poland; evacuation of British cities. 3 September — Britain and France at war with Germany

1940 April–May — Germany invades neutral Denmark and Norway. May — Germany invades neutral Holland and Belgium. May–June — British troops evacuated from Dunkirk. 10 June — Italy declares war alongside Germany. 17 June — France falls and seeks armistice. De Gaulle escapes to London. July–September — Battle of Britain. SOE formed. September — The Blitz on London begins

1941 June — Germany invades the USSR. December — Japan attacks USA at Pearl Harbor; now it is Britain and the Commonwealth, the USA and USSR versus Germany, Italy and Japan

1942 Germany invades unoccupied (Vichy) France. Russian counter-offensive begins at Stalingrad

1943 July — The Allies invade Sicily; fall of Mussolini. September — Invasion of Italy. Italy surrenders and joins the Allies

1944 June — The invasion of France. 1 August – The Warsaw Rising. 24 August — The Allies enter Paris, the Free French leading

1945 23 March — The Allies cross the Rhine. 30 April — Hitler commits suicide in his Berlin bunker. 8 May — Unconditional surrender of Germany. 6 & 9 August — Atom bombs dropped in Japan. 2 September — Japan surrenders

1946 January — SOE disbanded

Index

Further Reading

The Origins of World War 2 R. Parkinson (Wayland Documentary History Series, 1970)
Odette Jerrard Tickell (Chapman Hall, 1949)
Women in Wartime: The Role of Women's Magazines J. Waller (McDonald Optima, 1987)
All the Brave Promises Mary Lee Settle (Pandora 1984)
Out of the Cage (Women's experience in two World Wars) Gail Braybon and Penny
    Summerfield (Pandora, 1987)

Film

The Sorrow and the Pity, 1969
(Explores the complete relationship between the French and their German occupiers, and
    the Resistance.)

The publishers would like to thank the following for supplying illustrations for this book:

Barnaby's Picture Library 51; BBC Hulton Picture Library 10, 11, 14, 15; John Frost Newspaper Library 13, 23, 57;
Mr and Mrs G. Hallowes 47, 61; John Hillelson 37; Imperial War Museum 12, 21, 22, 24, 26, 36, 46; National Film
Archive Stills Library/© Weintraub Screen Entertainment 41; Popperfoto 9, 48, 53; Roger-Viollet 33, 35, 38;
Topham 6, 17, 18, 19, 29, 30, 55, 60, cover below